KENYA

Let's All Pull Together!

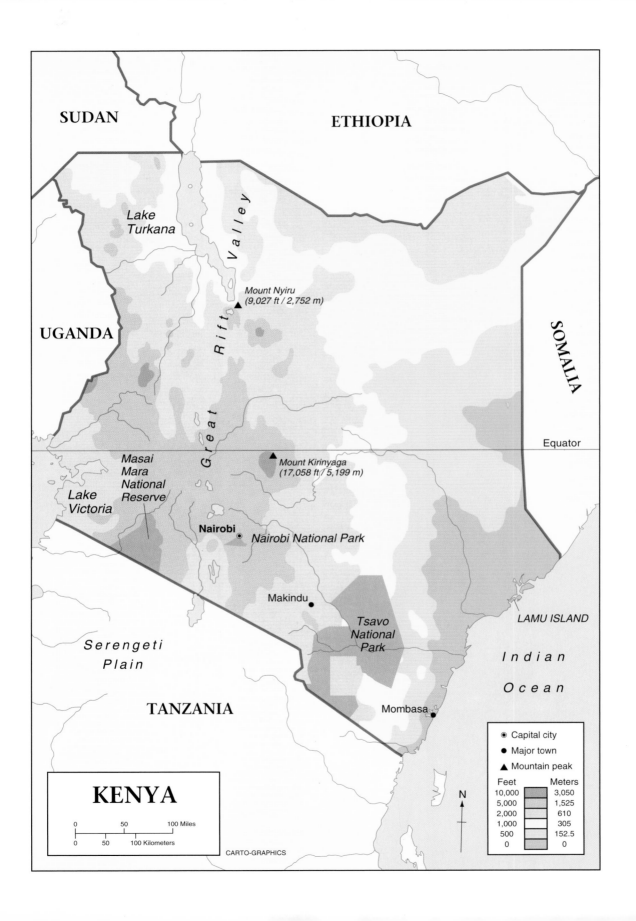

SUDAN

ETHIOPIA

*Lake
Turkana*

Great Rift Valley

UGANDA

SOMALIA

Mount Nyiru
(9,027 ft / 2,752 m)

Equator

*Masai
Mara
National
Reserve*

Mount Kirinyaga
(17,058 ft / 5,199 m)

*Lake
Victoria*

Nairobi

Nairobi National Park

Makindu

*Tsavo
National
Park*

LAMU ISLAND

*Serengeti
Plain*

*Indian

Ocean*

TANZANIA

Mombasa

⊙ Capital city

● Major town

▲ Mountain peak

Feet	Meters
10,000	3,050
5,000	1,525
2,000	610
1,000	305
500	152.5
0	0

KENYA

0	50	100 Miles
0	50	100 Kilometers

N

CARTO-GRAPHICS

EXPLORING CULTURES OF THE WORLD

KENYA

Let's All Pull Together!

David C. King

BENCHMARK BOOKS

MARSHALL CAVENDISH
NEW YORK

*The publisher would like to thank
Barbara Thomas-Slayter, director of the
International Development Program at Clark
University, for her expert review of the manuscript.*

Benchmark Books
Marshall Cavendish Corporation
99 White Plains Road
Tarrytown, New York 10591-9001

Library of Congress Cataloging-in-Publication Data
King, David C.
    Kenya : let's all pull together! / by David C. King.
      p.   cm. — (Exploring cultures of the world)
    Includes bibliographical references and index.
    Summary: Examines the geography, history, government,
people, and customs of Kenya,
    ISBN 0-7614-0393-0 (lib. bdg.)
    1. Kenya—Juvenile literature. I. Title. II. Series.
DT433.522.K57   1998
967.62—dc21   97-14448
                                            CIP

Printed in Hong Kong

Series design by Carol Matsuyama

Front cover: A Masai woman wears striking beaded jewelry.
Back cover: Elephants refreshing themselves at a watering hole.

Photo Credits
Front cover and page 50: Leo de Wys Inc./Bill Holden; back cover: Leo de Wys Inc./Bob Krist; title page and pages 9, 20, 24, 35, 38, 42, 47, 55: Bruce Dale/National Geographic Image Collection; page 6: AP/Wide World; page 6 (inset): Blackbirch Press Photo Archives; page 11: Medford Taylor/National Geographic Image Collection; page 12: Leo de Wys Inc./Richard Saunders; page 14: Bianca Lavies/National Geographic Image Collection; page 16: The Pierpont Morgan Library/Art Resource, NY; page 18: Frank & Helen Schreider/National Geographic Image Collection; pages 23, 45: George F. Mobley/National Geographic Image Collection; page 25: James L. Stanfield/National Geographic Image Collection; pages 28–29: ©Vision Impact/International Stock Photo; page 30: Leo de Wys Inc./Bill Bachmann; page 32: ©Catherine Ursillo/Photo Researchers, Inc.; page 37: Kenneth Love/National Geographic Image Collection; page 41: Volkmar Wentzel/National Geographic Image Collection; pages 48, 49: Leo de Wys Inc./W. Hille; page 52: ©Chad Ehlers/International Stock Photo; page 53: Courtesy of Kenya Tourist Office New York.

Contents

Kipchoge Keino became a national hero in 1968, when he captured a gold medal in the Summer Olympics and put his young nation on the map.

1
GEOGRAPHY AND HISTORY

Kenya Then and Now

A Race for His Country

A huge crowd had jammed into Mexico City's Olympic Stadium. It was the start of the 1968 Summer Olympic Games. As the athletes marched into the stadium for the opening ceremonies, there was little applause for the small team from Kenya. Many in the crowd had probably never even heard of Kenya; the African nation had been formed only five years earlier.

One of the Kenyan athletes was a runner named Kipchoge Keino. A member of the Kenyan police force, Keino had grown up running in the highlands of his homeland. He knew he could run fast. But how fast was he compared to the best athletes in the world? He was entered in the most important race in the Olympics—the 1,500-meter run, or "metric mile." And one of the men running against him in the event was the famous American track star Jim Ryun, who held the world record.

As the runners settled into their starting blocks, Keino thought about the people back home. He wanted to do well for them, not for just his family and tribal group, but for his new nation. There were only a handful of television sets in Kenya, all in Nairobi, the capital city. Transistor radios were everywhere, however, so he knew that many people would be listening to the event.

The starter's gun cracked, and the runners bounded forward. Keino found himself running smoothly and easily, stride for stride with the great Jim Ryun. He was not bothered by the thin air of Mexico City's mile-and-a-half-high altitude—the highlands of Kenya were just as high above sea level.

As the runners headed into the last turn, Keino stayed close to Ryun. Then, with a sudden burst, he surged past Ryun and felt the finish-line tape stretch and break across his chest. Keino had not only won the race, but he had set a new world record: 3 minutes, 34.9 seconds!

Later, standing on the podium to receive his gold medal, Keino had to choke back tears as the Kenyan national flag was raised for the first time in Olympic history. Half a world away, the radio relayed the news and the playing of Kenya's new national anthem. Fishing families on Lake Victoria shared the joy with farmers in the highlands, cattle herders on the grasslands, and office workers in Nairobi.

Keino went on to win a silver medal in the 5,000-meter run. His teammates won gold and silver medals in the 3,000-meter steeplechase. But it was that first gold in the 1,500 meters that electrified the sports world and filled Kenyans with a deep pride in their young nation. In a single race, Keino had proved that Kenyans could hold their own against the best in the world. That proud day was also the beginning of a great tradition: Since 1968, Kenyans have been among the world's most successful runners in the distance races.

Nature's Dramatic Contrasts

Kenya, about the size of the state of Texas, is wedged into the east coast of Africa. To the east lies the country of Somalia, to the north are Ethiopia and Sudan, to the west are Uganda and

Lake Victoria, and to the south is Tanzania. Kenya's short coastline stretches along the Indian Ocean. It is a land of amazing variety, including a huge area of grassy plains, or savanna. There are bamboo forests, rich farmland, thundering waterfalls, parched deserts, white sand beaches, and even snow-capped mountains. The plains cover about three-quarters of the land area. The tall grasses in the south give way to semidesert and desert in the north.

With the rich green highlands behind him, this Kenyan takes time out to relax.

Because the equator runs through the center of Kenya, we think of a climate that is sunny and hot. And it is, in many places. But a visitor can also stand almost on the equator and build a snowman! The reason for this oddity is that climate changes with altitude. The higher a place is above sea level, the cooler it is likely to be. So, the towering peaks of Mount Kirinyaga (once called Mount Kenya), Africa's second-highest mountain, are snow-covered all year, even though the mountain is almost on the equator.

Another striking feature of the country is the Great Rift Valley. This ancient trench of land cuts through Kenya from north to south. It begins far to the north, in the Middle Eastern nation of Lebanon, and stretches 4,000 miles (6,400 kilometers) south into southern Africa. This great valley is 50 miles (80 kilometers) wide and 1 mile (1.6 kilometers) deep. It cuts through the highlands of central and southwestern Kenya, which cover about one-quarter of the country. The highlands have a mild climate, plenty of rainfall, and good soil for farming. About 80 percent of Kenya's people live in this region.

Untamed Beauty and Few Cities

At dawn, a pink cloud rises slowly from a shimmering lake. Gradually, the cloud is seen to be made up of thousands of pink flamingoes taking flight. The thunderous sound of the birds' flapping wings can be heard for miles.

There is also thunder on the Serengeti Plain in Tanzania, as more than a million animals move across the savanna. There are great herds of hooved animals—zebras, wildebeests, African buffalo, a dozen species of antelope, and giraffes. Following along their flanks are the meat eaters—lions, leopards, cheetahs, hyenas, and wild dogs. These

These hippopotamuses are cooling off in a river in the Masai Mara National Reserve, one of the nation's many areas set aside for wildlife.

fierce predators are ready to pounce on any animals that stumble or stray from the herd.

This mighty movement is part of a great migration that takes place every year. The herds come to Kenya every May from the Serengeti. They are driven by some mysterious instinct telling them that there is fresh grass in the north. In November, the migration begins again, just as suddenly, this time to the south.

The vast savanna that Kenya shares with Tanzania holds the greatest concentration of wild animals in the world. It includes large herds of elephants. There are smaller groups of rhinoceros and hippopotamus. The ponds and shallow lakes are home to shorebirds and crocodiles. The trees are shared by chattering monkeys, colorful birds, and a variety of snakes, including the cobra and python.

Lush tea plantations like this one dot the highlands of central and southwestern Kenya.

To the people of Kenya, this immense collection of wildlife is an important part of their heritage. They feel a deep sense of responsibility for helping the wild herds to survive. No hunting is allowed in Kenya, and poachers—people who steal or kill the animals illegally—are dealt with harshly. More than forty national parks and game reserves cover almost 10 percent of the country. Tsavo National Park covers an area the size of the state of Massachusetts!

Some miles west of Tsavo, in Kenya's modern capital city of Nairobi, busloads of visitors can watch lions, zebras, giraffes, and other animals roaming free in Nairobi National Park. This park lies within sight of modern hotels and office buildings. Nairobi, with well over a million people, is Kenya's largest city. The only other large city in Kenya is the seaport of Mombasa.

Most Kenyans are not city dwellers. More than three-quarters of the people live in rural villages. Most farming villages are in the central and southwestern highlands. There, farm families grow tea, coffee, cotton, and sugarcane. Along the shores of Lake Victoria, many families live by fishing the shallow waters of the world's second-largest freshwater lake. Small tribes of Kenyans live by herding cattle, goats, sheep, and camels. Many of these groups are nomads—people who move often in search of fresh pasture and water.

From the Dawn of Time

Humans have lived in what is now Kenya for many thousands of years, perhaps longer here than anywhere else on earth. But we know almost nothing about the history of these people before 150 years ago. The earlier people left no written records. The remains of their societies have all but vanished.

Kenyan scientists are making plaster models of the skull of Australopithecus boisei, a near-human that lived more than a million years ago in the Great Rift Valley.

However, modern anthropologists—scientists who study early human life—have been fascinated by human remains found in the Great Rift Valley. Some of the most famous discoveries of early human skulls and bones were made by Mary and Louis Leakey, two Kenyans of European descent. Their findings in the 1960s and 1970s indicate that humans using stone tools were living in the valley more than one million years ago. These discoveries, and later ones by the Leakeys' son Richard, have led scientists to call the Great Rift

Valley the "Cradle of Humankind"—the place where human life first developed.

More than 2,000 years ago, groups who spoke Bantu languages moved into what is now Kenya. The rich soil for farming and good grazing land, plus the pleasant climate of the highlands, drew other groups as well. Some of these later groups were called Cushite. Others spoke languages known as Nilotic. Most of the Africans of modern Kenya are descended from one of these three groups.

The Influence of Asia and Europe

About 1,000 years ago, merchants from the Arabian Peninsula established trading posts along the coast of East Africa. These traders brought with them Arabic, their language, and Islam, their religion. That religion had begun with the Prophet Muhammad in the seventh century A.D. Followers of Islam are called Muslims. The Arabs mixed with the African population. The blending of the two cultures created a new language and culture, which became known as Kiswahili (key-swah-HEEL-ee), or simply Swahili. Kiswahili culture and the Islamic religion are still prominent today in the coastal towns. Kiswahili and English are the official languages of modern Kenya.

In 1498, the first Europeans arrived. Portuguese explorer Vasco da Gama was the first to land on the coast along the Indian Ocean. Others followed. For a time, the Portuguese dominated the rich coastal trade in gold and ivory. After a series of wars in the mid-1700s, the Kiswahili and Arabs regained control.

No Europeans ever saw the interior of Kenya until the mid-1800s. At that time, British explorers traveled to Lake

The Portuguese explorer Vasco da Gama was the first European to land on the coast of East Africa.

Victoria. They discovered it to be the source of the Nile, the world's longest river. The powerful nations of Europe then took control of almost the entire continent of Africa. They changed it into a patchwork of colonies ruled by Britain, France, Germany, and other countries. The British claimed Kenya.

The Emergence of Modern Kenya

The British government began ruling Kenya in 1895 and made it a "royal colony" in 1920. The colonial government invited British settlers to take over the best lands. There, the settlers established plantations for growing tea, coffee, cotton, and sugarcane. In the early 1900s, a railroad was built connecting the port of Mombasa with Lake Victoria. Nairobi was established as a

KENYAN GOVERNMENT

Kenya is officially a republic, a kind of government in which authority comes from the people. Much of the nation's power, however, rests in the hands of President Daniel arap Moi.

The government has three branches: executive, legislative, and judicial. The president is the head of the executive branch. He chooses a vice president and a cabinet of ministers who manage government departments. These officials are selected from the legislative, or law-making, branch, called the National Assembly. It has 202 members; 188 are elected and 14 are appointed. Elections are held at least every five years. They can be held earlier under certain circumstances. Every citizen of Kenya can vote at age eighteen. In the judicial branch, the highest court is the Kenya Court of Appeals. It is made up of a chief justice and four justices. The second-highest court is the High Court. There are numerous lower courts.

Kenya is divided into seven provinces, made up of districts, plus the district of Nairobi. Each province is governed by a commissioner appointed by the president. Nairobi is governed by a city council.

railroad construction camp. Soon it grew into a city and was made the capital of British Kenya.

The people of Kenya's many tribes could not stop the British from taking over their lands. Their spears were no match for the guns of the British. In addition, the tribes consisted of many different ethnic groups. They found it impossible to unite against the Europeans. By the 1920s, many of the people were forced to work as laborers on the British plantations or as servants in the beautiful homes of the plantation owners and merchants. Nairobi was fast growing into a modern city, with elegant houses, restaurants, theaters, and clubs. But Africans found that they were not allowed in these places—except as servants. The British built roads and hospitals. Church missions established schools. But most of Kenya's 7 million or 8 million people hated being controlled by about 30,000 British.

Slowly, the people of Kenya found ways to unite against British rule. A turning point came after the end of World War II (1939–1945), when a powerful man named Jomo Kenyatta returned to Kenya. He had been away from Kenya for a long time. He quickly became the leader of the independence movement. When the British refused to consider independence, some Kenyans turned to violence. They formed an organization called the Mau Mau. This resistance group used terrorist tactics in their struggle for Kenya's independence in the 1950s. Kenyatta opposed the violence, but the British blamed him for it. In 1952, he was arrested, and in 1953 he was sent to prison.

Jomo Kenyatta led Kenyans in their struggle for independence and became the first president of the new nation.

The British finally managed to put down the Mau Mau uprising. The long struggle, however, helped convince them that Kenya could not be held as a British colony much longer. In 1961, Kenyatta was released from prison. Two years later, the nation was granted its independence. As the Kenyan flag was raised above the capital city in a solemn ceremony, a huge crowd shouted, *"Uhuru! Uhuru!"* (ooh-HOO-roo)—the Kiswahili word for "freedom."

The Struggle for Democracy

In 1964, Kenya formed a republic, with Jomo Kenyatta as its first president. He encouraged the British to stay. Some of them did. He also included members of many different tribal groups in his government. Kenyatta tried to create national unity by allowing only one political party, the Kenya African National Union, or KANU. There were still free elections, but political parties based on the many tribal groups were not allowed. Through the 1960s and 1970s, Kenya's new government worked, and the young nation enjoyed a period of amazing economic growth and prosperity.

When Kenyatta died in 1978, people realized that much of their progress was owed to his powerful personality. The man who became the next president, Daniel arap Moi, became more and more powerful, especially after an attempt was made to overthrow his government. People who opposed him were arrested, and opposition publications were banned. Moi was finally forced to hold elections. He was re-elected president in 1992, but opposition to him has continued to grow throughout the nation. The majority of Kenyans remain committed to the idea of democracy and continue to hope that it will be a reality one day soon.

A woman from one of Kenya's many tribal groups smiles hello as she pokes her head out of her home.

2
THE PEOPLE

Who Are the Kenyans?

When the national flag is raised or lowered anywhere in Kenya, everyone stops to watch the brief ceremony. Kenyans are proud of their independence. Their flag is an important symbol of the national unity that they are working toward. Kenyans belong to more than forty different ethnic groups, or tribes. Each group has occupied the same territory for centuries. And each has its own language and customs. One of the greatest challenges facing the government of Kenya is creating a sense of loyalty to the nation that is stronger than the peoples' loyalty to their tribes.

Many Cultures, Many Languages

Almost 99 percent of Kenya's 28 million people are native Africans. The rest are of Arab, Asian, and European descent. The largest of the native groups, the Kikuyu (key-KOO-yu), number more than six million. They make up about 22 percent of the total population. The Kikuyu are farmers who live in the southwestern highlands. Another group are the Luo (LOO-oh), who make up about 15 percent of the nation's

SAY IT IN KISWAHILI

Here are a few common words and phrases in Kiswahili:

Hello.	*Jambo.* (JAHM-bo)
What's new? What's happening?	*Habari gani?* (ha-BAH-ree GAH-nee)
Things are good. We are fine.	*Nzuri.* (en-ZUR-i)
Everything is peaceful.	*Salama.* (sa-LAHM-ah)
We will see each other again.	*Tutaonana.* (Toot-ah-oh-NANAH)
Sleep peacefully (Good night).	*Lala Salama.* (LA-la sa-LAHM-ah)

Gestures can convey as much as words. People show approval with both thumbs up. Pointing with a finger is rude. If you want someone to come, you gesture with all the fingers of the right hand. When speaking to someone, it's important to look directly into the person's eyes.

population. The Luo farm and fish on the shores of Lake Victoria.

There are many other farming groups scattered through the highlands and the coastal plain. Smaller groups, like the Masai in the southern savanna, and the Somali in the dry lands of the north, live as nomadic herders. They move with their cattle whenever they need fresh pasture or water.

The many tribal groups speak different languages. Although some of these languages are similar to one another, communication between the groups has been a major obstacle to national unity. To try to overcome this problem, Kiswahili was made the official language of Kenya in 1970. Because it is similar to many tribal languages, Kiswahili has been easy for the different groups of people to learn. English is also an official language. It is widely used in business, education, and government. Many Kenyans continue to use their tribal language at home, though.

Life in the Country

Almost 80 percent of Kenya's people live in the countryside. Their way of life differs from group to group. The Kikuyu are Kenya's most prosperous tribe. Their trim, mud-walled houses are scattered across the fertile highlands near Mount Kirinyaga. The door of every house faces the mountain. The Kikuyu believe the Supreme Being lives on Mount Kirinyaga.

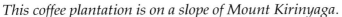

This coffee plantation is on a slope of Mount Kirinyaga.

Kikuyu farmers use modern methods to grow tea and coffee, which are sold throughout the world. They grow wheat, beans, sweet potatoes, and other crops for their own needs. The Kikuyu also raise cattle and goats.

Along the shores of Lake Victoria, the Luo live in more crowded villages and towns. Most Luo are farmers, but many families make their living by fishing. These families go out on the lake in small, single-sail boats called *dhows*. They bring in daily catches of big Nile perch, which are sold in nearby towns or shipped by train to Nairobi.

Nomadic Herders

The way of life of nomadic tribes like the Masai presents a sharp contrast to the settled life of the Kikuyu and Luo. The Masai live much as they have for centuries, herding cattle on the dry grasslands of southern Kenya. These tall, slender people were once feared as the bravest warriors in all of Africa. Until recently, a young man of the Masai tribe had to show his courage by going on a lion hunt alone. The Masai herd their cattle across great distances, and they pay little attention to whether they have crossed the nation's border with Tanzania.

Far to the north, in the parched land around Lake Turkana, smaller tribes like the Turkana and Rendille (REHN-dil-lee) also live as nomadic herders. While the Turkana raise cattle, the Rendille keep herds of camels, sheep, and goats as well. The modern ways of life that are transforming much of Kenya have hardly touched these groups. Their homes are made of the branches of acacia trees and wild sisal—a plant used for making mats and baskets. Grazing land is so scarce that herders may travel twenty-five miles a day to find food

After a day on the water, a fisherman brings in his nets.

and water for herds that have as many as 1,000 animals. While they will trade with traveling merchants for such things as cloth or beads for jewelry, the Rendille, Turkana, and similar groups have little interest in modern products.

Still other groups follow a way of life between the extremes of the nomads and the settled farmers. The Samburu,

A Samburu tribesman herds cattle during the dry season.

for example, live near the dry lands of the Rendille, but their homeland is in the foothills of Mount Nyiru. There they enjoy more abundant rainfall and a milder climate. The Samburu herd animals, but they also grow crops. They move their herds only during the driest season.

City Life

One hundred years ago, Masai herders watered their cattle at a spring they called *enkare nyarobe*, the Masai words for "sweet water" or "cool water." The only reminder of that watering hole is the name of the city of Nairobi. It was here that the British built a railroad construction camp in 1896. Today, it is the capital of Kenya and by far the largest city. Nearly two million people live in Nairobi.

Downtown Nairobi is modern and bustling. There are beautiful high-rise hotels, office complexes, and apartment buildings. Many of the people who crowd the stores and restaurants are dressed in styles that would not look out of place in New York, London, or Paris. Cars, buses, and trucks clog the tree-lined streets. Restaurants, movie theaters, and concert halls offer evening entertainment.

The people of Nairobi represent nearly all of Kenya's many tribal groups. While the Kikuyu and Luo have in the past held many of the best jobs and government positions, other groups are now represented as well. Nairobi residents work in government offices, banks, stores, and a few food-processing plants.

While much of the city is modern and prosperous, there is another Nairobi on the outskirts. The people there struggle against poverty. This part of Nairobi is made up of shantytowns—a jumble of shacks built out of wood scraps,

Nairobi, Kenya's capital city, has a modern skyline. A hundred years ago, it was the location of a watering hole for Masai cattle.

cardboard, and tin. Nairobi's shantytowns grew as thousands of people flocked to the city. They hoped to find jobs and a better standard of living. Newcomers to Nairobi face a hard time until someone in the family manages to find work. Government efforts to build more low-cost housing have not been able to keep up with Nairobi's growing population.

Kenya's seaport city of Mombasa is the second largest city. It is only about one-fourth the size of Nairobi. Mombasa

Although most of Kenya's Muslims live in the north or along the coast, this beautiful mosque is in Makindu, an inland city in the south.

is one of Kenya's oldest communities. It dates back to the time of the first Arab traders, 1,000 years ago. The Arab influence is still evident. Many Mombasans are Muslims. They dress as Muslims do in Arab cities. The women wear long dresses, and cover their faces with veils. The men dress in white tunics and trousers.

A Mixture of Religions

In the mid-1800s, Christian missionaries from Europe began to work in Kenya. They converted many people to Christianity. The missionaries also established schools and hospitals. Today, about 70 percent of Kenyans are Christians. A little more than half belong to Protestant churches and the remainder to the Roman Catholic Church.

Within the Christian churches, there is much variety in the way religion is practiced. Many of the churches are independent of the official Roman Catholic Church and the various Protestant churches. Priests and ministers in these churches often mix Christianity with traditional African beliefs. The spiritual leader of an independent church, for example, might recognize the tribal belief that spirits live in trees, rocks, animals, or other natural objects. It is estimated that there are almost 300 of these independent churches scattered throughout Kenya.

Along Kenya's seacoast and in the northeast, there are large numbers of Muslims. They make up about 7 percent of the total population. The Muslims worship in mosques, rather than churches, and they observe the Muslim calendar of holy days. The rest of Kenya's people, nearly one-quarter of the population, practice the tribal religions they have followed for centuries.

In the countryside, where this Masai family lives, everyone has chores to do.

3

FAMILY LIFE, FESTIVALS, AND FOOD

The Kenyan Way of Life

Children growing up in any of Kenya's rural communities know everyone in their village. Many of their neighbors are members of their extended family—the large family unit that includes grandparents, aunts, uncles, and cousins. Children feel so close to their extended family that they sometimes call their aunts "mother" and their uncles "father."

Kenyan children also feel close ties with other people in the village because they are members of the same tribal group. Members of a tribe have a strong sense of responsibility to help one another. The elders, or older members of the village, meet often to settle disagreements and to discuss common concerns. If one family has a serious problem, the elders will look for ways to help. One of the challenges modern Kenyans face is finding ways to keep these tribal and family ties strong as more and more villagers move to Nairobi or one of the fast-growing towns.

Tradition and Change

In the country, where more than three-fourths of the people live, every member of the family contributes to its well-being. Children as young as five or six have tasks, such as gathering firewood or tending goats. Men and boys lead the cattle to pasture. In farming communities, they work in the fields. Women and girls carry water, repair and clean the hut, make clothes, cook, and often tend a vegetable garden. Evenings are usually spent around the dying embers of a fire or around a kerosene lamp. This is a quiet time for talking, telling stories, and singing.

If anyone in the extended family needs help, other family members provide it. In cattle-herding groups, for example, if someone's herd becomes too small, other family members will give up some of their cattle. In a similar way, if a family lacks the money to send a son or daughter to secondary school, an uncle may provide the funds.

When even one family member moves to the city, however, it becomes difficult to keep up this system of help. According to tradition, for instance, aging parents are to be cared for by the youngest adult son. However, he may be miles away, in Nairobi, searching for work.

Many people feel that the ever-increasing movement of people to the city is loosening family ties and destroying valuable tribal traditions. But there are also advantages to city life. For many Kenyans, a city job means a higher standard of living and perhaps a way to give financial support to the family back home. In addition, the city offers new opportunities to women. By the mid-1990s, for example, one-third of Kenya's college students were women. And women make up 40 percent of the urban workforce.

Time to Celebrate

When Jomo Kenyatta was president of Kenya, he would frequently address crowds wearing an elegant leopard skin robe over his business suit. At some point in his speech, he would shout the Kiswahili word *harambee* (ha-RAAM-bay), meaning, "Let's all pull together." And thousands of people would chant the response, *"Harambee! harambee!"*

Since that time, one of the greatest national festivals is celebrated every year on October 20. It is called Kenyatta Day, which is also know as Harambee Day. In Nairobi, the day is celebrated with a great parade. The parade ends in front of 50,000 people who are crowded into the National Stadium. Groups come from all over Kenya to take part in the festival.

Dressed in his leopard skin robe, Kenyatta reviews the troops.

Schoolchildren march with their teachers, or else in groups of Boy Scouts or Girl Guides. Dancers come from many different tribal groups. They perform in colorful costumes topped with elaborate headdresses shaped like birds or animals. Then, as air force jets roar overhead, Kenya's small national army and band march into the stadium, dressed in flame-red tunics and tall hats made of black and white fur.

Kenyatta Day is also celebrated in towns outside of Nairobi. Buildings are decorated with bunting, and the day is spent in feasting, singing, and dancing. Other national holidays are observed in a similar way, including *Madaraka* on June 1, which marks the founding of the republic. *Jamhuri,* or Independence Day, is celebrated on December 12.

Ancient Celebrations

While national holidays are important, every tribal group spends far more time celebrating its traditional festival days. Among the Masai and other nomadic tribes of southern Kenya, for example, the most joyous time of year comes in April. This is the beginning of the rainy season. The Masai gather in large camps from miles around to celebrate the time for moving their herds of cattle to the fresh grass and sparkling streams of the Great Rift Valley. Their feasting, singing, and praying for healthy herds lasts for several days. Dancers perform for hours, accompanied by people playing handmade drums and flutes. The dancers dress very colorfully. Their hair is dyed red, their bodies are decorated with black stripes, and they wear headdresses made of ostrich feathers and sometimes even a lion's mane.

In the southwestern highlands, the Kikuyu celebrate the start of the planting season with feasts, music, prayer, and

Members of a Masai tribe dance at a celebration.

dance. The festivities last for several days. Some of the dancers are warriors. They wear robes of leopard or zebra skin. Their faces and bodies are dyed blue and decorated with white body paint. Carrying spears and shields, these Kikuyu warriors dance to express pride in the strength of their tribe.

Weddings are causes for celebration everywhere. North of the southwestern highlands, in the semi-desert homeland of the Turkana, people gather from as far away as one hundred miles to celebrate a wedding. The bridegroom's family pays a "bride price" of several head of cattle to the bride's family. The young couple are the center of attention for eight days of feasting, music, and dance.

A Variety of Foods

The foods of Kenya are as varied as the land and the people. Each region and tribal group has its own style of cooking. The variety of available foods is even greater in the cities and towns.

One of the foods that is common throughout the country is a cornmeal mixture, somewhat like mashed potatoes, called *ugali*. It is used to make *uji*, a thick porridge. Among the breads found in many regions are *chapati*, a flat bread, and a fried bread called *kitumba*.

Among the Kikuyu, the evening meal is likely to be *ngombe* (en-GOHM-bay), a barbecued beef, and *irio*, a dish made of potatoes, peas, and corn mashed together. In Luo country, near Lake Victoria, a common evening meal includes a fish dish called *tilapia*, usually Nile perch in a spicy tomato

At outdoor markets like this one, shoppers can choose from the many kinds of tropical fruit grown in Kenya.

KISWAHILI FRUIT SHAKE

Ingredients:

1 pint milk

1 scoop vanilla ice cream

3 tablespoons shredded coconut

1/2 teaspoon vanilla flavoring

1 banana

Place the milk, ice cream, coconut, and vanilla in a blender or mixing bowl. Peel the banana and cut it in thin slices. Add the banana to the mixture. With an electric mixer, blender, or egg beater, whip the mixture thoroughly to create a thick, frothy milk shake. Serve it right away. This makes enough for two refreshing glassfuls.

sauce. As a side dish, the Luo often serve *githeri*, a mixture of red beans and corn.

In Nairobi and along the coast, Kiswahili cooking is popular. It is quite different from the foods of other regions. A favorite Kiswahili meal is a meat stew made with shredded coconut and coconut milk. A side dish eaten with this might be *matoke*—corn mashed with banana or plantain, a banana-like fruit. People in Nairobi, Mombasa, and large towns also enjoy British-style foods, such as hamburgers or fish and chips (French fries). Many city restaurants are owned by Asian Kenyans whose ancestors came from India. Indian meals served at these restaurants frequently include rice and savory curry sauces.

Most nomadic peoples drink a lot of milk and eat dairy products such as yogurt. They also eat wild berries and honey. Vegetables are usually regarded as "cattle food." Meat is reserved for special festivals.

Fruit juices, milk, and bottled soft drinks are all popular in Kenya. Coffee is a common drink, but Kenyans prefer *chai*, a tea that is boiled with a lot of milk and sugar. Desserts often consist of Kenya's many fresh fruits, including bananas, pineapples, papaya, mangoes, and oranges. Yogurt and ice cream are popular in towns and cities. And roadside vendors sell a variety of snacks, such as roasted corn, meat on skewers, sodas, and *mandazi*, a sweet doughnut.

Clothing: Modern and Traditional

In the country, as well as the city, most Kenyans wear clothing styles that are similar to those worn in Europe and North America. Men wear shirts and trousers. Business suits are common in the cities. Women normally wear knee-length dresses or skirts and blouses.

There are variations on these European and American styles, however, especially among women. One of the most common items of women's clothing is a long piece of colorful cotton fabric called a *kanga*. A *kanga* can be wrapped around the waist and worn as a skirt. It can also be used as a shawl or as a head covering during rainstorms. Mothers often tie a *kanga* over one shoulder and use it for carrying infants on their backs. Many women also wear head scarves. Somali women cover their heads with brightly colored shawls.

The people of the nomadic tribes wear traditional clothing. Among northern tribes, like the Boran and Turkana, women wear a garment called a *gorfa*. Traditionally, a *gorfa* is made from several panels of goatskin or sheepskin that have been sewn together and dyed red and black. The *gorfa* is wrapped around the body one and a half times and secured with a leather thong and a rope belt. Since inexpensive

This young Masai wears the splendid jewelry and orange toga that are traditional in his tribe.

cotton cloth has become more available throughout Kenya, these wrapped garments are now often made of red and black cotton.

Men and women of almost every group are fond of jewelry. Necklaces made of many rows of beads are the most popular item. Bracelets and earrings are also common.

Many Kenyan students are eager to learn and grateful to have the chance to go to school.

4

SCHOOL AND RECREATION

The Desire
to Learn

A fourteen-year-old boy of the Pokot tribe had hitched a ride on a truck headed for a market town. As the truck rumbled past other Pokot boys herding their cattle, the boy leaned out the window and shouted, "I'm going to school! I'm going to school!" The nearest secondary school was in the town, 50 miles from his home. Three days later, the discouraged boy was back home. The school was full, and there was no place for him to live.

The boy's story reveals two important points about education in Kenya. The first is that most Kenyans feel that education is very important. They believe education will help them to improve their lives. The second point is that there are not enough schools—especially secondary schools—for the people living in the northern half of the country.

Before Kenya won its independence from Great Britain, there were few schools for native Africans, except those run by the church missions. Since 1964, the government has spent large sums to build schools and train teachers. The population of Kenya is growing so fast, though, that progress has been slow. In spite of the problems, more and more Kenyan children are completing at least primary school.

Ways of Learning

A group of twenty-eight Masai children gather beneath an acacia tree for the start of primary school. There is no school building. Instead, the students crowd onto two long wooden benches. The boys are dressed in shorts and blue shirts. The girls wear red tunics over blue blouses. There are few books and paper is scarce. But the children don't seem to notice. They are excited to be there and eager to learn.

School is not compulsory in Kenya, but more than 80 percent of the children now spend at least three years in primary school. Primary school, which begins at age six, continues for seven years. Only about half of Kenya's children complete all seven years. The first three years of school are free; after that, there is a small tuition charge. Only about one teenager out of seven manages to go on to high school. Many of those who complete the four years of high school go on to college. They attend the University of Nairobi, or they go to smaller colleges that train people for jobs in teaching, health care, or business.

Because the government cannot provide enough schools or teachers, private groups have stepped in to help. With funds raised from church and civic groups throughout the world, these groups have established what are called self-help, or *harambee*, schools. Volunteers from Europe and the United States help bring schooling to even the most remote regions of the country. There are now more *harambee* high schools than government-operated high schools.

Primary-school children pose for a picture outside their school in the country.

The lessons for rural children, like the Masai students, are taught in Kiswahili for the first three years, and then in English. Many of the lessons are about practical matters, such as how to tell time and how to practice good personal health and hygiene. In addition to a government-paid teacher, older members of the tribe provide lessons in, for example, how to keep cattle healthy, how to find fresh water, and how to survive a drought. Other elders teach tribal stories, songs, and dances. Still others teach crafts, such as wood carving or basket making. The regular teacher gives lessons in academic subjects: reading, writing, and math.

Students in Nairobi are taught in English throughout the primary grades. The subjects they learn are much like those taught in other places in the world: reading, writing, geography, math, history, and science.

Kenyans are proud of their progress in education. About 70 percent of the people are now literate—that is, they can read and write. This is a remarkably high percentage for a newly independent nation.

Fun and Games

Although children outside of the cities have important work to do when they are not in school, there is plenty of time to play. Even while herding cattle, Kenyan boys find time for foot races, wrestling matches, and spear-throwing contests.

Both boys and girls play a variety of games—either traditional games or ones they invent themselves. There are several games requiring pebbles or seeds. One of these games involves tossing a number of small stones in the air and trying to catch them on the back of the player's hand. Another, called *bao* or *ajua*, is similar to board games American children play. But Kenyan children use a homemade board and polished stones as game pieces.

Many of the games involve a lot of joking and laughing. Several girls, for example, will sit in a line with their legs stretched straight out. The leader taps along the row of knees, chanting something like "eenie, meanie, miny, moe." The last girl tapped must fold a knee under. This continues until all the knees are tucked under. Then, at the leader's signal, everyone stands up. If a girl's knees crack, she is one of the winners. If a girl's knees don't crack, everyone laughs and teases her, and she then becomes the leader for the next round.

Many young people join the Boy Scouts or Girl Guides.

There are also more than 1,000 wildlife clubs scattered throughout the country. Through these clubs, children learn how they can help preserve Kenya's famous wildlife.

46

Sports and Recreation

Soccer is Kenya's most popular team sport. There are soccer clubs even in the smallest towns. Pick-up games on any flat piece of land are common. Kenyans are especially proud when the national team, made up of players from many tribal groups, plays well against teams from other countries. In urban areas, tennis and golf are becoming increasingly popular. Cricket, learned from the British, is played as well.

Kipchoge Keino and other distance runners of the late 1960s established track and field as a major sport. Kenya did not compete in the 1976 Olympics, however, as a protest against the racial policies of South Africa. The country also boycotted the 1980 Games in Moscow, to protest the Soviet Union's invasion of Afghanistan. Beginning in the 1988 Olympics, Kenyans once again displayed their great abilities in distance events. Kenyans have won gold medals in the

Rugby, a sport brought to Kenya by the British, is still being played.

A clean and beautiful beach along the Indian Ocean attracts sunbathers, swimmers, and sailors.

800-meter, 1,500-meter, and 3,000-meter steeplechase, and the 5,000-meter run. Throughout the country, it is now common to see young men training along the mountain slopes in the hope of making the next Olympic team.

In Nairobi and the larger towns, people enjoy going to movies, concerts, plays, and dance performances. Recreation in the countryside is more traditional. Storytelling and riddles are popular, and singing and dancing are part of every celebration. While television is still limited to urban areas, transistor radios are used everywhere. Radio also gives people of every tribal group the chance to hear recordings of their traditional music. They gain an appreciation for the music of other groups, too.

5

THE ARTS

Tribal Treasures
and National Unity

When Kenya gained its independence in 1963, many Kenyans wondered how a feeling of national pride and unity could be created out of more than forty tribal groups. "We have no national identity," a journalist wrote. "What does the music of Kenya sound like? Where is our national literature? Every tribe has its own [arts and crafts], and none of it can be called Kenyan."

Only gradually did people come to realize that there does not have to be one single Kenyan culture. Instead, the richness of Kenya's arts lies in their diversity. Each group's arts, stories, music, dance, and crafts contribute something special. When the contributions of all the groups are mixed together, the arts of Kenya emerge as a colorful patchwork, rather than a single fabric.

A Kaleidoscope of Crafts

Of all their handcrafts, Kenyans are best known for their wood carving. Many of these intricate carvings serve a religious purpose. Small charms, or amulets, are used to protect a person from evil spirits or to attract helpful ones. Larger carvings of heads, human figures, or animals are often designed to represent gods or spirits. Examples of these outstanding wood sculptures are on display in museums and galleries throughout the world.

Shoppers look over a selection of handmade pots and baskets at one of Kenya's many open-air markets.

Over many centuries, each tribe and region developed its own style of carving. Some of the most unusual examples of the craft are made on the island of Lamu off the Indian Ocean coast. Lamu looks like a place forgotten by time. It is an ancient town, established by Arab traders 1,000 years ago. To preserve its unique atmosphere and history, Lamu does not allow cars or trucks on the island. Along its narrow, walled streets, houses are huddled close together. Every house is graced by a beautifully carved door. These world-famous doors are only one example of the skills of Lamu's woodcrafters. The carvers also make elaborate chests, stools, candlesticks, and models of the ancient sailing *dhows* that still ply the coastal waters.

Intricate woodcarvings decorate many everyday items.

Every town in Kenya has an open-air market twice a week where people engage in lively bargaining over the variety of handcrafts produced in that region. At the markets, and in Nairobi shops (where prices are fixed), people can buy wood carvings, jewelry, beautiful baskets made of sisal or dried grasses, and the colorful, handmade *kangas*. There are also handmade musical instruments, including drums, flutes, and stringed instruments.

The craft that shows most clearly the varied artistic tastes of the tribal groups is jewelry making. Men as well as women of nearly every group wear lots of jewelry, and they are highly skilled at making necklaces, bracelets, anklets, armlets, and rings for fingers, toes, and ears. In many tribes, a woman's status in society is indicated by the jewelry she wears. Among the nomadic Rendille, for example, an unmarried girl wears a necklace of up to twenty strands of white beads. A married woman wears an ornate headband and an elaborate necklace of copper wire and beads that may have thirty or more strands. When Rendille men marry, they wear a thick, round earring.

Jewelry is made from many different materials: semi-precious stones, copper, glass, amber, scraps of steel or aluminum, animal tails, and plastic. While the people of the Muslim tribes wear little or no jewelry, others vie with the Rendille for the most colorful decorations. The Pokot and the Masai, for instance, favor necklaces made of many rows of brightly colored beads. Some Turkana are known as "giraffe women" because their necks are stretched by massive strands of heavy beads.

Music and Dance

Every national holiday, and every family or tribal celebration, is an occasion for music and dance. Traditional Kenyan music is polyrhythmic, or made up of different rhythms. A single dominant rhythm is usually supplied by drums, the most common instrument. At the same time, woodwind or string instruments play a different rhythm. Singers chant or sing in a third rhythm. The result is a complex mixture of sounds that is often difficult for people from Western nations to follow.

A member of the Mbere tribe plays the drum at a celebration.

PRESERVING TRIBAL TRADITIONS

A number of organizations are working to preserve the traditions of the many tribal groups. They are also trying to help Kenyans understand that these traditions are part of their national heritage.

The Bomas of Kenya is a professional dance group that performs traditional tribal dances. The Bomas are constantly learning more about the dance forms of each tribal group.

The African Heritage Gallery, located in Nairobi, collects and exhibits examples of arts and crafts from Kenya's tribal groups.

The Kenya Cultural Center, also in Nairobi, includes the National Theater and the Theater School. The school teaches people to write and stage plays for public performances.

The Kenya National Museum works with the university to promote research into tribal history, music, folktales, arts and crafts, and religious practices. The museum's exhibits range from the earliest human fossil finds to displays of tribal lifestyles today.

Dances vary with each tribal group. Many dances are part of a religious ceremony. Warriors in elaborate costumes and headdresses dance for strength against their enemies. A mixed group of men and women in traditional costumes dances for an abundant rainy season, bountiful crops, or healthy cattle. Unmarried girls perform a ritual dance designed to bring them healthy families. All of the dance movements are complex and athletic. Some require acrobatic skill.

The people of Kenya are also fond of the music of Europe and North America. The Nairobi Orchestra plays the music of famous European composers, from Bach to Stravinsky. Modern jazz and rock music are played in city discos and nightclubs. Kenya's single radio station plays all kinds of music, including the music of the tribal groups.

Literature and Art

As more and more people move from the countryside to Kenya's cities and towns, many Kenyans fear that something of vital importance is being lost. The urban dwellers are losing touch with tribal traditions, such as stories, music, and dance. The stories that communicate so much of each tribe's wisdom seem particularly precious. These stories are *oral* folktales. They are kept alive by being told over and over. A single tribe may have thousands of these folk stories. Since the tribal groups have no written language, the stories could eventually be forgotten as Kenya becomes more urbanized.

To preserve as many of the oral tales as possible, some Kenyans are writing them down in Kiswahili or English. Playwrights and novelists are exploring the theme of urban life and the loss of tribal identity. A famous novel that contrasts the city with the country is *Petals of Blood* by Ngugi wa Thiongó (en-GUH-ji way thi-ONJ-oh).

While none of the tribal groups has a long tradition of painting, modern artists are creating paintings and murals. The work of Elimo Njau (El-LEE-moh en-JOW) is popular for its expression of Kenya's national hopes and aspirations, even though he grew up in Tanzania. One of Njau's most outstanding works is a large mural depicting the heroic struggle for independence. It is in the Muranga Memorial Chapel, on the outskirts of Nairobi.

Country Facts

Official Name: *Jamhuri ya Kenya* (Republic of Kenya)

Capital: Nairobi

Location: Kenya is located on the east coast of Africa. It is bordered on the north by Ethiopia and Sudan, on the west by Uganda and Lake Victoria, and on the south by Tanzania. Somalia lies to the east, and the Indian Ocean to the southeast.

Area: 224,961 square miles (582,650 square kilometers). *Greatest distances:* east–west, 560 miles (901 kilometers); north–south, 640 miles (1,030 kilometers). *Coastline:* 300 miles (483 kilometers).

Elevation: *Highest:* Mount Kirinyaga, roughly in the center of Kenya, 17,058 feet (5,199 meters). *Lowest:* sea level.

Climate: Although Kenya is located on the equator, the climate varies a great deal with altitude. The coastal region is hot and humid all year. In the highlands, where most of the people live, temperatures average 67° F (19° C). The annual rainfall is 40–50 inches (102–127 centimeters). The plains areas are drier and become semi-desert and desert in the north.

Population: 28 million. *Distribution:* 24 percent urban; 76 percent rural.

Form of Government: Republic

Important Products: *Natural Resources:* gold, limestone, timber, salt, sapphires, garnets. *Agriculture:* coffee, tea, sugarcane, cotton, beef cattle, corn, wheat, rice, cassava, and fruit (bananas, coconuts, mangoes, oranges, papaya, plantains). *Industries:* tourism, processed foods, textiles, chemicals, oil refining.

Basic Unit of Money: shilling; 1 shilling = 100 pence

Language: Kiswahili (also called Swahili) is an official language, as is English. There are more than forty tribal languages and dialects.

Religion: 70 percent Christian (37 percent Protestant, 33 percent Roman Catholic); 7 percent Muslim; 23 percent traditional tribal religions.

Flag: The national flag has three horizontal stripes: black, representing the people of Kenya; red, for the struggle for independence; and green, for agriculture. In the center of the flag is a red shield covering two crossed spears, symbolizing the defense of freedom.

National Anthem: *Ee Mungu Nguvu Yetu* ("Oh God of All Creation")

Major Holidays: New Year's Day, January 1; Easter (date varies); *Madaraka* Day, June 1 (the establishment of the Republic in 1964); Kenyatta Day, October 20 (honoring the day Kenyatta was arrested by the British); *Jamhuri* (Independence Day), December 12; Christmas, December 25; Boxing Day, December 26 (a British holiday, now used for visiting family and friends). Muslims celebrate the month of Ramadan and other holy days in their calendar.

Flag of Kenya

Kenya in the World

Glossary

amulet: a small carved figure, or charm, used to attract good spirits or ward off evil ones

anthropologists: scientists who study the origins and development of human life

dhows: slender sailing canoes that have been used for centuries on Lake Victoria and the coastal waters of the Indian Ocean

ethnic group: a group that shares the same language and customs

gorfa: a traditional garment worn by women in northern nomadic tribes. It is made of several panels of animal skin or cotton, sewn together, and wrapped around the body.

harambee (ha-RAAM-bay): a Kenyan saying that means "Let's all pull together"

harambee **schools:** also called self-help schools. They are organized by private groups and communities to help provide education in remote areas.

highlands: the hilly fertile region of southwestern and central Kenya where the majority of Kenyans live

Islam: the religion founded by Muhammad in Saudi Arabia in the seventh century A.D. People who follow Islam are **Muslims,** and they believe that there is one God ("Allah" in Arabic) and that Muhammad is his prophet.

kanga: a colorful piece of cotton fabric worn by many Kenyan women as a skirt; also used for other purposes, such as a sling for carrying a baby

Kiswahili: also called Swahili, the official language of Kenya; the name for the culture that emerged on the Kenyan coast, a mixture of Arab and African peoples

Mau Mau: a violent uprising during the struggle for independence in the 1950s, causing thousands of deaths; also the name for the fighters in the uprising

Muslim: a follower of the religion of **Islam**

nomads: people who have no permanent home but move from place to place in search of food and fresh water and pasture for their animals

polyrhythmic: music consisting of two or more rhythms played or sung at the same time

safari: a trip into the national parks and game reserves of Africa

savanna: a generally dry region of grassland and scattered trees

sisal: a plant used for weaving mats and baskets; a major crop in Kenya

For Further Reading

Bailey, Donna, and Sproule, Anna. *Kenya*. Austin, TX: Raintree Steck-Vaughn, 1990.

Burch, Joann J. *Kenya: Africa's Tamed Wilderness*. New York: Dillon Press, 1992.

Griffin, Sandra. *Family in Kenya*. Minneapolis, MN: Lerner Publications, 1988.

Haskins, Jim. *Count Your Way Through Africa*. Minneapolis, MN: Lerner Publications, 1989.

Jacobsen, Karen. *Kenya*. Chicago: Children's Press, 1991.

King, David C. *Dropping in on Kenya*. Vero Beach, FL: Rourke Book Co., 1995.

Pateman, Robert. *Kenya*. New York: Marshall Cavendish, 1994.

Stein, R. Conrad. *Kenya*. Chicago: Children's Press, 1985.

Index

Page numbers for illustrations are in boldface

About the Author

"One of the great things about books is that they can carry us to every corner of the world. We can also travel back in time, visiting people and places from recent years or the distant past. I hope you enjoy this book's journey across both space and time," says David C. King.

Mr. King is a historian and an author, who has written more than thirty books for young readers. In addition to books about foreign countries, he has written stories and biographies in American history. He and his wife, Sharon Flitterman-King, live in the village of Hillsdale, New York. They welcome visitors.